Memories of the Railway from Didcot to Banbury

The signalbox on the platform at Aynho station in the days of the Great Western Railway.

Lamplight Publications

Brief History of the Line

The progress of the railway from the Thames Valley up the Cherwell Valley has its complications. The Act for the GWR had included Oxford in its ambitions, so with the completion of the main line to Bristol in the famous 7ft ¼ inch broad gauge an Oxford Railway was established in 1841. This was for a branch with a junction connection at Didcot. Consequently the first Oxford station was opened at Grandpont on June 12, 1844. The Oxford road coach to London ceased in 1841.

Complications arose with proposals north to Banbury, originally called Oxford & Rugby, with another scheme called Oxford, Worcester & Wolverhampton. Both schemes became involved in acrimonious relations with the 'narrow' 4ft 8½ inch London & Birmingham Railway. The conflict is covered in MacDermot's *History of the Great Western Railway*. The upshot was that the Rugby line was abandoned just north of Fenny Compton and extended by a new Birmingham & Oxford Railway to Birmingham in 1852.

The station at Banbury was opened on September 2, 1850. Branches sprouted to Abingdon (June 2, 1856); to Thame (October 24, 1864); to Witney and Fairford (November 14, 1861; 1873); a junction at Aynho (July 1, 1910) for a new shorter route from Princes Risborough to compete with the Euston - Birmingham route of the LNWR with two-hour expresses. Also a branch to Chipping Norton (April 6, 1887.).

The extension schemes brought the GWR north of the River Thames to a new station site occupied as the present, this opened on October 1, 1852.

On August 13, 1900 a line of eight miles was put in north of Banbury connecting with the new Great Central Railway at Culworth. On July 1, 1902 this brought about a series of valuable through services including Newcastle-on-Tyne to Bournemouth via York. Coaches were provided by the GCR whilst engines hauling these trains were GWR, GCR and LSWR. Also through coaches Manchester - Banbury - Oxford - Reading - Guildford - Redhill and Dover.

A large engine shed was built at Banbury opened on October 6, 1908 to accommodate through passenger and goods workings.

The era of the GWR is beyond comparison in its appeal, with the Brunswick Green and sparkling brass of their engines hauling long trains of chocolate and cream livery coaches with drifting clouds of white steam ascending the vally slopes. A number of stations and bridges along the line were built in the local pale limestone which must have made them stand out very distinctly against the rich pastures of the alluvial plane.

With nationalisation in 1948 the railways began to be reduced as the common carrier of all things, in later years confirmation of this came with the building of motorways. The M40 motorway was built in the valley in 1991. Increasing closure affected only five stations on the main line but all closed for goods facility. Thereby much of the railway of former years has now gone but what remains continues successfully with park and ride facilities. Occasionally a steam special emerges from Didcot or Tyseley and for a few moments images from the past rematerialise.

Published by Lamplight Publications
260 Colwell Drive,
Witney,
Oxon OX28 5LW

First Published 2007

ISBN: 978 1 899246 19 9

Printed and bound at
The Alden Press,
De Havilland Way,
Witney,
Oxon OX29 0YG

Didcot on April 11, 1958 with 4096 *Highclere Castle* piloting 5002 *Ludlow Castle* leaving with the 13.18 from Paddington to Weston-Super-Mare. The new signalbox was opened in December 1931; it was closed in May 1965.

B W L Brooksbank

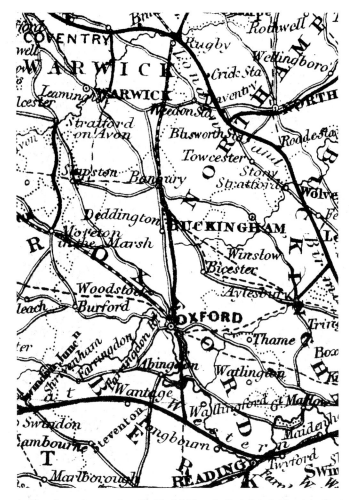

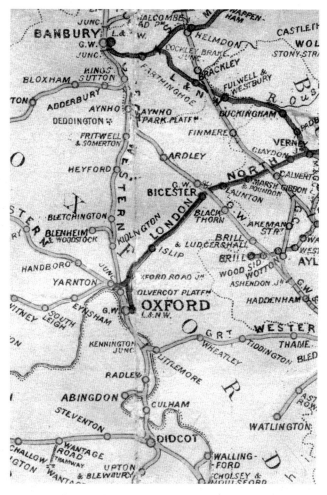

The route largely under construction in 1846, note that it is laid out to the town of Rugby, the original name of the railway.

It must be noted also that the map shows lines proposed at that time but not built. For example a line is shown proposed from Aylesbury to Oxford, the original intention of the Aylesbury Railway. In fact this never proceeded beyond Aylesbury and the two county towns were never to have direct rail connection.

Bill Simpson Collection

The thirty six miles fom Didcot to Banbury with connecting lines as in 1923. Most routes are those of the GWR with the darker marked being those of the LNWR. The connection between the two north of Oxford was borne out by some defection by a company called the Oxford, Worcester & Wolverhampton Railway that entered an agreement to run their trains across this way to Euston on April 1, 1854. By process of amalgamations the defecting company was eventually absorbed by the GWR but the route continued to be used for goods trains.

Bill Simpson Collection

From 1961 hydraulic diesels were introduced on the Western Region working on the main line to the west. One of the 'Western' class is seen here heading for Paddington. This photograph also shows the Didcot Provender store that was demolished in 1967. Also a part of the Didcot Transfer Shed used for exchanges between gauges, a reason that became redundant as the broad gauge receded west.

Brian Sessions

On July 25 1963 7025 *Sudeley Castle* takes the east curve avoiding the station with an 'up' train to Paddington from Hereford. The curve of 1 mile 2 chains was installed in 1860 to provide standard gauge connection when the station was still broad gauge, the station was converted to mixed gauge in 1863.

K C H Fairey

One of the then comparatively new Inter-City HST passing through Didcot to Paddington in 1983.

Bill Simpson

In 1967 Didcot became the home of the Great Western Society at Didcot Railway Centre continuing the life of the locomotive shed. Since that time the site has flourished and 14XX class no 1466 was the first to arrive seen here with its appropriate push-pull coach as a shining example of that success. It first steamed again in preservation in 1966.

Bill Simpson

A Hereford - Worcester - Paddington express passing through Culham hauled by no 7027 *Thornbury Castle* on Tuesday, July 23, 1963. The footbridge is superbly vintage GWR.

Andrew Bratton

Looking south at Culham in the 1960's the station has survived as a rare example of the Brunel Tudor style design for intermediate stations. In reality a station representing the age of the original broad gauge making it of unique historical value. The grassey area on the left was the horse dock and milk landing platform. The space in front of that is where the signalbox once stood.

A Smith

The GWR opened a halt for Appleford village on September 11, 1933. It is seen here looking down from the road bridge in 1964 towards Didcot.

S Smith

A special diesel unit train operated on June 30, 1984 between Oxford and Abingdon. It is seen here approaching Radley in the afternoon of that day. The day was made all the more evocative by the beautiful summer sunshine typifying the favourite images of a country branch line. Radley station opened on September 1, 1873.

Bill Simpson

Oxford in the early 1960's with obvious traffic intensity. The unrebuilt West Country class no 34103 *Calstock* at the platform line is probably about to make an imminent departure, possibly with the *Pines Express*. After then the 9F 2-10-0 on an oil train will be released from it patient waiting. Going in the opposite direction the new 47 class diesel in green is looking to proceed under the far 'down' line signal. Oxford station was rebuilt in 1971 and again with a footbridge in place of a subway in 1990.

Brian Sessions

Traffic movements north of Oxford station on September 28, 1963. The two-coach 1.25 SO all stations to Moreton-in-the-Marsh has just left the bay platform which is why the signals are holding the pannier tank on the adjoining 'down' line. At the same time Stanier 2-8-0 48527 brings in a train of mineral wagons, possibly from the Bletchley - Oxford line. Mechanical signalling ceased at Oxford on October 13, 1973.

Peter Baughan

In the 1970's Oxford Publishing Co organised quite a number of local rail tours and some not so local. Here two class 31 diesels nos 31209 and 31285 are arriving at Oxford on the morning of Sunday, September 17, 1978 to collect its passengers. The train was called the *Welsh Valleys Rambler* and travelled up and down a number of colliery branches in south Wales.

Bill Simpson

Twilight Intercity at Oxford with HST awaiting to proceed to Worcester at 6.55 on a Winter evening in 1993.

Bill Simpson

Kidlington station in the mid-1960's looking rather untidy as the station closed to passengers on November 2, 1964. The bay on the right was used by trains serving the Woodstock branch and the cattle dock. What vintage worth now the derelict Standard Vanguard? Just north of Kidlington at Shipton-under-Wychwood a terrible accident took place on December 24, 1874 when a coach that had been added at Oxford became derailed. As the coach was closest to the engine when the enginemen realised this they applied the brakes with disasterous results of crushing the coach between them and the train.

Lens of Sutton

Bletchington station c1965 an improved design from the original with cantilevered roof and buildings of the early 20 century period. The original station was timber with a hipped roof.

A Smith

No 7912 *Little Linford Hall* passing Bletchington on a Bournemouth - Newcastle through train on Saturday, August 10, 1963. One of the popular through workings made possible by the Banbury - Culworth link with the Eastern Region.

Andrew Bratton

The station at Bletchington on March18, 1955. Through the arch of the roadbridge can be seen wagons on the Shipton-on-Cherwell cement works siding. Note the bridge support set well back allowing space required in the broad gauge period. A building on the left beyond the bridge was an early water tank house.

Bill Simpson Collection

Tackley Halt looking towards Oxford, this was opened on April 6, 1931 on the 72¾ milepost. There was once a signalbox just north of Tackley Halt which was removed in 1950.

Lens of Sutton

Platform view looking towards Oxford on the extreme curve at Heyford forced by the hill and location of the canal and river. It required a line speed of 60 mph which was sorely tested in steam days by impatient enginemen trying make up time!

H C Casserley

The station in 1950's with the signalbox visible. The lattice footbridge has recently been replaced with an effective but less attractive steel plate bridge.

Lens of Sutton

Heyford in 1980 not long before the building was removed. The stations along the line were provided with a set of very strong but attractive limestone buildings built shortly after the days of its construction. As the locally quarried stone matched with the the road overbridges this must have made the line very attractive in early days. A matching shelter was provided on the 'up' platform also. The Oxford Canal of 1790 runs closely alongside the station which for the observant provides an interesting juxtaposition of the early road bridge over the canal, now a footpath.

Bill Simpson

Fritwell by the canal with a goods train heading towards Banbury on Saturday, February 1, 1964. It is a view that recalls the pleasure of observing steam locomotives working on a high level. The photograph was taken in a time when much of the line was in open vista in the valley but this view like so many others is overgrown and obliterated.

Andrew Bratton

Fritwell & Somerton station, a modest timber structure added to the line in September 1854. More lightly built as it is situated on an embankment close to Somerton village. Fritwell village is quite some distance away towards Bicester. Originally it was called 'Somerton Oxon' until 1906 when it was changed to the final title. This view taken on Saturday February 1, 1964, the station closed on November 2 of the same year.

Andrew Bratton

A 'County' class 4-6-0 1015 *County of Gloucester* passing slowly through Aynho station with an 'up' freight on Tuesday September 4, 1962. Aynho was the place of the first accident on the line on October 20, 1852.

Andrew Bratton

A fine study from GWR days as 2981, one of the 'Saint' class, passes through Aynho on June 8, 1939. The first of the class was withdrawn in 1931, the last in 1953.

H C Casserley

A 3-car set W51402; 59512; 51360 plus suburban coach forming the 11.29 am to Oxford from Banbury at Aynho for Deddington station on Thursday Sept 4, 1962. Recalling the early days of the diesel multiple units painted in olive green with the 'cats whisker' livery. The embankment of the 1910 direct line between Aynho and Princes Risborough is clearly visible in the background.

Andrew Bratton

The platform Halt at Aynho on the high level was opened in 1910. It had no more than four stopping trains daily and was closed on January 7, 1963. On this view a single unit no W55002 calls with the 11.15 am to Princes Risborough from Banbury on Tuesday, September 4, 1962.

Andrew Bratton

A King class 4-6-0 *King Richard III* passing Aynho Park Station with Wolverhampton to Paddington passenger train on Tuesday, September 4, 1962. The new line of 1910 allowed this famous class to run on Birmingham expresses as they were restricted from the Didcot route by their weight at Oxford. New bridge work at Oxford has now enabled them to use this route also.

Andrew Bratton

As mixed traffic locomotives the 'Hall' class would be equally utilised on freight or passenger. Here 4-6-0 4959 *Purely Hall* on an 'up' freight near Kings Sutton at 5.00pm on Thursday 30, 1964.

Andrew Bratton

A class 56 heads south at Aynho with a container train in 1991. At this point the River Cherwell and Oxford Canal combine courses as one crosses the other. The Cherwell Valley has many attractive settings and there is always a great deal of water providing a haven for many wild creatures.

Bill Simpson

Essential in steam days, 7008 *Swansea Castle* picks up water as it heads a Paddington - Banbury stopping train over Aynho troughs Monday July 22, 1963.

Andrew Bratton

On Sunday, March 24, 1963 no 4093 *Dunster Castle* passing Kings Sutton at speed with a Birmingham to Paddington express. This station was closest to the junction for the Chipping Norton branch which closed on June 4, 1951. On May 6, 1968 this station was reduced to an unstaffed Halt.

Andrew Bratton

Passing through the imposing little station of Kings Sutton, which opened on December 1, 1873, no 6930 *Andersey Hall* with a Wolverhampton - Ramsgate train on Saturday July 27, 1963.

Andrew Bratton

Kings Sutton with 6929 *Warton Hall* on a Margate train at 12.40 pm on Saturday July 27, 1963. All that now remains of these impressive buildings is the 'down' side shelter.

One of the Castle class 4-6-0's no 7011 *Banbury Castle* heading a Birmingham - Oxford train south of Kings Sutton Thursday July 30, 1964.

Andrew Bratton

A photographic opportunity to record the progress of the fastest steam locomotive in the world passing through Kings Sutton in 1987. This being A4 4-6-2 *Mallard* no 4468 on a journey to Birmingham.

Bill Simpson

Banbury GWR station as it appeared at the turn of the century. An all over roof design by Brunel that was built in larger form at Oxford. The building was demolished in the rebuilding of 1956-8 when a new 'down' relief line was added.

Banbury MPD with 6917 *Oldlands Hall* on October 10, 1965. It is truly amazing to realise the size of the installation at Banbury of which not a thing remains.

Andrew Bratton

In the modern age of complete unit trains it now seems archaic that once the engines used a turntable to turn around to take up another journey. But Banbury had a large installation for engines just south of the station on the 'down' side. It is being made use of by one of the large goods engine 2-8-0's no 3820 at Banbury MPD on Sunday September 22, 1963.

Andrew Bratton

An unusual steam engine profile on Banbury shed, former LNER A1 class 4-6-2 60145 *Saint Mungo* on Sunday, September 5, 1965. This was a Warwickshire Railway Society special from Birmingham to Eastleigh, Bournemouth and Weymouth. At Banbury the engine was replaced by 7029 *Clun Castle*.

Andrew Bratton

North of Bridge Street Road bridge at Banbury as 60145 approaches with the enthusiast special from Birmingham September 5, 1965.

Andrew Bratton

It seems as if many different types of railway engines appeared on Banbury shed, here 'Royal Scot' class no 46156 named *South Wales Borderers* is receiving preparation for duty on Saturday June 20, 1964.

Andrew Bratton

The fastest steam locomotive in the world together with one of the most famous; north of Banbury in 1987 A4 4-6-2 no 4468 *Mallard* and 4-6-2 no 4472 *Flying Scotsman*. A chill in the air helped create this large cloud of exhausting steam as the pair began to accelerate their progress north. The first 'Shakespeare' special ran from Marylebone to Stratford-upon-Avon on February 3, 1985 and was hauled by no 4498 *Sir Nigel Gresley*.

Bill Simpson

Throughout the 1980's there was a remarkable flourish of steam returning to Banbury with specials each weekend and sometimes during the week to Stratford-upon-Avon 'The Shakespeare Limited' from London Marylebone, a round trip dining special for tourist interest. It was an experience unlikely to be repeated as Marylebone can no longer accommodate steam locomotives and the line through the Chilterns is now heavily used by Chiltern Railways. Yet for a time it seemed that the clock had been turned back just a little bit bringing a highly evocative experience to those that witnessed it. Such a train is visible here with no 35028 *Clan Line* a rebuilt Merchant Navy class bringing one of the specials into no 1 platform at Banbury.

Bill Simpson

Before the official end of steam on British Railways many steam specials were run and on March 4, 1967 Ian Allan Publisher promoted two specials from Paddington. One to Birkenhead 'The Birkenhead Flyer' via Didcot from where it was hauled by 4079 *Pendennis Castle* to Chester where 73026 took the train forward to Birkenhead. The other to Birmingham Snow Hill, Wolverhampton Low Level, Shrewsbury and Chester. This was hauled by 7029 *Clun Castle* and called 'Zulu'. It travelled over the Princes Risborough, Bicester route with *Clun Castle* taking over at Banbury. It is seen here in apparent adulation by the people of Banbury and a professional cameraman. In the distance Banbury's new station buildings of some ten years.

Quainton Railway Society Archive Collection